$\mathcal{P}$ARKWOOD

PARKWOOD

STEPHANIE BEATTY AND SUSAN GALE HALL

Cataloging in Publication Data

Beatty, Stephanie, 1948–
    Parkwood

Includes bibliographical references.
ISBN 1-55046-300-4

I. Parkwood (Oshawa, Ont.). 2. McLaughlin family. I. Hall, Susan Gale, 1952–
II. Title.

FC3099.084Z57 1999   971.3'56   C99-930615-4
F1059.5.084B34 1999

Published in 1999 by
BOSTON MILLS PRESS
132 Main Street
Erin, Ontario NOB 1T0
Tel 519-833-2407
Fax 519-833-2195
e-mail books@boston-mills.on.ca
www.boston-mills.on.ca

An affiliate of
STODDART PUBLISHING CO. LIMITED
34 Lesmill Road
Toronto, Ontario, Canada M3B 2T6
Tel 416-445-3333
Fax 416-445-5967
e-mail gdsinc@genpub.com

Distributed in Canada by
General Distribution Services Limited
325 Humber College Boulevard
Toronto, Canada M9W 7C3
Orders 1-800-387-0141 Ontario & Quebec
Orders 1-800-387-0172 Ontario & Other Provinces
e-mail customer.xctvice@ccmailgw.genpub.com
EDI Canadian Telebook S1150391

Distributed in the United States by
General Distribution Services Inc.
85 River Rock Drive, Suite 202
Buffalo, New York 14207-2170
Toll-free 1-800-805-1083
Toll-free fax 1-800-481-6207
e-mail gdsinc@genpub.com
www.genpub.com
PUBNET 6307949

    03   02   01   00   99   1   2   3   4   5

FRONT COVER: THE PARKWOOD ESTATE, FORMER HOME OF ROBERT SAMUEL AND ADELAIDE MCLAUGHLIN, 1917–1972. *[PA]*

BACK COVER: SAM MCLAUGHLIN AT PARKWOOD IN 1954, IN A 1908 MCLAUGHLIN MODEL F, ONE OF THE FIRST AUTO-MOBILES MADE IN CANADA. *[PA]*

Text and cover design by Mary Firth
Authors' photograph on back cover by Andy Cole, Sunset Studios
Printed in Canada

This book was a volunteer project created to benefit Parkwood.

THE CANADA COUNCIL | LE CONSEIL DES ARTS
FOR THE ARTS | DU CANADA
SINCE 1957 | DEPUIS 1957

We acknowledge for their financial support of our publishing program the Canada Council, the Ontario Arts Council, and the Government of Canada through the Book Publishing Industry Development Program (BPIDP).

CONTENTS

PARKWOOD IN WINTER. *(PA)*

INTRODUCTION

A VISIT TO PARKWOOD, the former home of Sam and Adelaide McLaughlin and their family, affords a rare glimpse into the past. Because the interior and gardens remain much the same as they were in the 1930s, it appears as if the McLaughlins are still in residence. Oshawa's National Historic Site is significant not only for the McLaughlin family connection, but because it is one of the last grand estates in Canada associated with prominent architects, craftsmen and landscape architects of the inter-war period.

When built in 1917, Parkwood was the most expensive house in Canada. Additions in the 1930s further enlarged the home from forty to fifty-five rooms. The imposing L-shaped mansion, from which the McLaughlins played an important role in Canada's business and social life for fifty-five years, sits on twelve distinctively landscaped acres and is open for tours year-round.

THE McLAUGHLIN FAMILY

"The family always said I had wheels in the head."

ROBERT SAMUEL MCLAUGHLIN was born to Mary Smith and Robert McLaughlin on September 8, 1871, in Enniskillen, Ontario. One of five children, Sam had three older siblings: John James (Jack) (1865), Mary Jane (1867) and George (1869). Elizabeth, born in 1874, was the youngest. Sadly, their mother, Mary, died of tuberculosis in 1877, leaving Robert to care for the young family. Within a year he had remarried, providing his children with a stepmother, Sarah Jane Parr.

Sam was said to be the liveliest of his siblings. His brother George's daughter, Dorothy McLaughlin Henderson, characterized him in her 1972 book: "Sam was quick, spontaneous, adventurous. He was a go-getter." An older Sam was fond of telling the story of when he was five years old, and a wheel drying in the loft of his father's carriage works fell on his head. "The family always said I had wheels in the head," was how he liked to recount the accident. By the time Sam was seven years old, his father had moved the family to the nearby bustling town of Oshawa. Robert McLaughlin's plan was to expand his growing venture, the McLaughlin Carriage Company, a business he had founded in 1867, the year of Canada's Confederation.

SAM AND BROTHERS AND SISTERS, 1878. [ML]

IN THE 1880S THE BICYCLE was a popular mode of transportation, and Robert purchased a penny farthing model for Sam. Perhaps he felt this would be a good outlet for Sam's energy. Sam was soon riding great distances, frequently travelling to Toronto and back, about sixty kilometres, in one day. Once Sam even took a holiday cycling from Oshawa to Brockville and back. He enthusiastically entered bicycle races in fairs and meets, and did so well, a family joke was that when he married he would be able to furnish a house with all the pickle dishes, cruets and cups he won. Sam's response to the jibe was "I was going to be too busy to be anything else but a bachelor."

SAM MCLAUGHLIN IN HIS LATE TEENS. (MH)

LIFE WAS NOT ALL RACES AND FAIRS. In 1887, having finished high school in Oshawa, Sam joined his father and older brother George in the thriving family business. In a 1954 *Maclean's* magazine article, Sam recalled: "I became an apprentice in the upholstery shop. I soon found that George had not been exaggerating when he said it was no advantage to be the boss' son. I swept the floors and did all the other menial work that apprentices have hated from time immemorial. Everybody in those days worked a fifty-nine hour week except the bosses (and, I soon discovered, the boss' son). They sometimes worked seventy or eighty hours, without overtime either." His weekly wage was three dollars, of which his father kept all but fifty cents for room and board. Sam was determined and hardworking and by 1892 he was a partner with his father and brother George in the McLaughlin Carriage Company.

ROBERT, SAM AND GEORGE MCLAUGHLIN, BUSINESS PARTNERS. *(MH)*

"The only person I really saw in the church that day was a vision of beauty in the choir."

rebuilt. The new house included sleeping porches and verandahs. The one-acre property had a small swimming pool, orchards and facilities for horses and ponies. During this time the McLaughlin daughters attended public schools in Oshawa. After the move to Parkwood, the three youngest were tutored at home by a teacher who lived in residence on the third floor.

ABOVE LEFT: ADELAIDE LOUISE MOWBRAY. *(MH)* ABOVE RIGHT: ROBERT SAMUEL MCLAUGHLIN, CIRCA 1898. *(MH)* BELOW: KING STREET EAST, CIRCA 1908. FOUR MCLAUGHLIN DAUGHTERS SITTING IN A RED CUTTER BUILT BY SAM. THE SAME CHILD-SIZE CUTTER IS ON DISPLAY AT PARKWOOD. *(PA)*

ON A SUMMER SUNDAY IN 1897, Sam bicycled out to the small village of Tyrone to visit his uncle on the old family homestead. He was invited to church with his uncle's family. There, he noticed a young schoolteacher in the choir. Her name was Adelaide Louise Mowbray, and Sam would later say, "The only person I really saw in the church that day was a vision of beauty in the choir." On their second date Sam proposed, and by February 1898, they were married.

Daughters Eileen (1898), Mildred (1900), Isabel (1903), Hilda (1905) and Eleanor (Billie) (1908) were born when the family lived on King Street East in Oshawa. After the original house burned down around 1910, the girls resided with friends while the house was

OPENING OF THE OSHAWA HOSPITAL AUG 13 1910

OSHAWA GENERAL HOSPITAL WAS FOUNDED IN 1910, THANKS IN PART TO THE FUNDRAISING EFFORTS OF ADELAIDE MCLAUGHLIN. PARKWOOD IS LOCATED SOUTH OF THE HOSPITAL ON ALMA STREET. THE MCLAUGHLINS GENEROUSLY SUPPORTED THE COMMUNITY BY GIVING TWO HOUSES TO THE HOSPITAL: PARKWOOD AND THE PROPERTY AT 138 KING STREET EAST. (NM)

Later, Sam said of Adelaide, "She has been a wonderful helpmate always and possesses great charm not only for me but for all who know her." Betty McMullen, Adelaide's secretary, also remembers her as a talented public speaker. Sam was proud of the role Adelaide played in their public life and relied on her to compose and deliver numerous speeches at a variety of functions.

She was clever, very proper, and had considerable organizational skills. Adelaide led a fundraising drive to open the Oshawa General Hospital in 1910 and was the president of the Ladies Auxiliary of the hospital for over fifty years. She also founded the Home and School Association in Oshawa and was active in the Girl Guide Association.

© 1983

THE 1908 MODEL F MCLAUGHLIN BUICK WAS
MANUFACTURED IN OSHAWA, ONTARIO, BY THE
MCLAUGHLIN MOTOR CAR COMPANY. THERE WERE 154
MADE, AND THEY SOLD (AS ILLUSTRATED) FOR $1,750.
A MODEL F IS ON DISPLAY AT THE CANADIAN
AUTOMOTIVE MUSEUM IN OSHAWA. [CAM]

THE TURN OF THE CENTURY brought rapid changes, and Sam resourcefully shifted his business interests to the new "horseless carriages." Until the First World War, people had relied on horsedrawn buggies for transportation, but automobiles were quickly replacing carriages. The motor car was the future, and Sam was determined to be a participant in the burgeoning automobile industry. Of his first drive in a car, he commented: "After a few miles at the controls of this one-cylinder, chain-driven juggernaut, I had a new kind of wheels in my head — motor-driven wheels."

By 1908 he was president of the newly formed McLaughlin Motor Car Company, with his father retaining the presidency of the McLaughlin Carriage Company. Buicks and Chevrolets were successful money-makers for the McLaughlin Motor Car Company, but by 1915 the McLaughlin Carriage Company was losing business. In December 1918, General Motors bought out the McLaughlin Motor Car Company. Sam and George retained a substantial interest in GM of Canada with Sam remaining as president of the new company.

THE
McLaughlin
family, circa
1913–1915. Back
row: Mildred
and Eileen.
Front row:
Adelaide,
Eleanor (Billie),
Hilda, Sam,
Isabel. (MH)

THE HOUSE

Prospect Park was the perfect site to build a larger, more elegant home.

NINETEEN FIFTEEN WAS AN IMPORTANT YEAR for Sam and Adelaide. The flourishing family business enabled them to purchase a central Oshawa property known as Prospect Park, some fourteen acres then operated as a popular amusement park.

In 1840, John B. Warren owned the site and built a wooden house upon it. The following owner, William Henry Gibbs, tore down the Warren house and built a lavish home he called Prospect House. When Gibbs went bankrupt in the early 1880s, the property was sold to Colonel Mulligan. In 1902, it was elaborately landscaped and converted into an amusement park by the new owner, Eli S. Edmondson. The property was subsequently purchased by the McLaughlins in 1915.

Sam and Adelaide planned to tear down the existing house and construct a home to reflect their growing affluence. Darling and Pearson, a prestigious architectural firm, was engaged to design a palatial estate, including a main house and several outbuildings. By March 1916, final blueprints were complete and construction soon started. It was reported in the *Oshawa Times* in 1967 that "Because of the war, Col. McLaughlin thought it best to stop construction on Parkwood. But reports say that Oshawa Council advised him to carry on because if work stopped, local men would be out of jobs." The newly named Parkwood was completed in 1917 at a cost of $100,000, and was then the most expensive house in Canada.

The architectural firm Darling and Pearson rarely designed houses, but made an exception for the McLaughlins. The new Centre Block of Ottawa's Parliament Buildings and Toronto's Royal Ontario Museum were two of the firm's well-known commissions.

A STAFF OF FORTY was employed to maintain this elegant estate. Staff included a secretary for Adelaide, three chauffeurs, a Scottish butler, cooks, maids, and as many as twenty gardeners. In later years a nurse was hired for Sam. The chauffeur and butler lived in cottages across the street from Parkwood. The head gardener resided in the gatehouse, unmarried maids stayed on the third floor of the house, and workmen lived above the garages.

ABOVE: PARKWOOD'S EXTERIOR IS CLAD IN ROUGH, TAUPE-COLOURED STUCCO, WITH GREEN-BLACK SHUTTERS ON THE WINDOWS. STATELY CORINTHIAN COLUMNS MAKE A DRAMATIC ENTRANCEWAY THROUGH WHICH VISITORS PASS INTO THE FIFTY-FIVE ROOM, L-SHAPED MANSION. *(PA)*

BELOW: THIS EVOCATIVE PICTURE IS POSSIBLY OF ELEANOR (BILLIE), SAM AND ADELAIDE'S YOUNGEST DAUGHTER, TAKEN SHORTLY AFTER THE MOVE TO PARKWOOD. LATER, STARTING IN 1936, THE MCLAUGHLINS SPENT MOST WINTERS AT CEDAR LODGE, THEIR HOME IN BERMUDA. *(PA)*

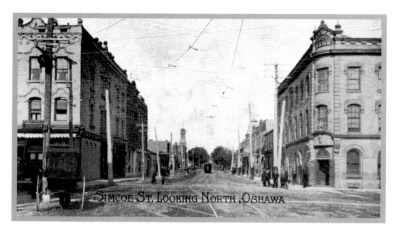

SIMCOE ST. LOOKING NORTH, OSHAWA

ABOVE: VISITORS TO PARKWOOD COULD FOLLOW THE STREETCAR TRACKS NORTH ON SIMCOE STREET. BEYOND THE TREES, ON THE WEST SIDE, THEY WOULD ARRIVE AT THE IMPOSING PARKWOOD GATES. (NM)

BELOW: LOOKING SOUTH ON SIMCOE STREET. PARKWOOD GATES ON THE RIGHT, CIRCA 1920. (PA)

THE PARKWOOD ESTATE is in the centre of this photograph, surrounded by the mature trees so loved by Sam McLaughlin. To the right of Parkwood, Simcoe Street runs north and south. The apartment building on the east side of Simcoe Street is the site of George McLaughlin's former home. Oshawa General Hospital (Lakeridge Health Corporation) sits north of the mansion, its parking garage on the northwest corner of the existing estate. The Formal Garden is south of the parking garage.

Extending from the north side of the main house is the flat-roofed recreational wing, containing the squash courts, pool, barber shop and bowling alley. Young male guests of the McLaughlin daughters stayed in the "bachelors quarters" above the barbershop and to the left of the tall greenhouse. The greenhouses are located at right angles to the recreational wing.

AERIAL VIEW OF PARKWOOD AND THE HOSPITAL, AFTER 1975. [OGH]

NINETEEN FORTY-ONE MARKED the completion of a ten-year period of additions and renovations to the house and gardens. Darling and Pearson, the original architects, designed significant changes, including the enclosure of the loggia, a large sunroom addition on the south side, and the renovation of verandahs to create the breakfast room. Adelaide, with the help of a British interior decorator and John Lyle, a Toronto architect, redecorated many rooms during the 1930s and early 1940s to give the house a lighter, less formal atmosphere.

ABOVE: THE NEW SUNROOM BECAME THE CENTRE OF ACTIVITY IN THE MCLAUGHLIN HOUSEHOLD. *(PA)*

RIGHT: PARKWOOD IN 1919, BEFORE THE SUNROOM ADDITION. *(PA)*

THE LOGGIA WAS A
SCREENED AND
GLASSED-IN
SUNPORCH BEFORE
THE SUNROOM
ADDITION. AFTER THE
ADDITION, IT WAS
FREQUENTLY USED
FOR SCREENING HOME
MOVIES. [PA]

"Where is everybody?"

VISITORS WERE WELCOMED into the imposing, two-storey foyer, which boasted a cantilevered staircase and a rare aeolian pipe organ. Silk-covered panels line the stairway wall, concealing the organ pipes. For the entertainment of guests, Eileen would play the instrument herself, but Sam proudly played it as a player piano. It was capable of playing up to ten player rolls in sequence. All of the McLaughlin daughters played musical instruments. Hilda fondly remembers that they had a little orchestra of sorts, with Mildred and Hilda playing a duet on piano, Isabel on xylophone, and Billy performing percussion duties.

"WHERE IS EVERYBODY?" HILDA MCLAUGHLIN FONDLY RECOLLECTS THAT HER FATHER, SAM, WOULD SHOUT THIS GREETING AS HE CAME THROUGH THE FRONT DOOR AFTER A WORKING DAY IN THE OFFICES OF GENERAL MOTORS. THIS IS AN EARLY PHOTO OF THE FRONT HALL. *(PA)*

LEFT: IN THE 1930S,
A WROUGHT-IRON
BANISTER WAS MADE IN
FRANCE FOR
PARKWOOD, REPLACING
THE EARLIER, WOODEN
ONE. THE GARDEN
MURALS UNDER THE
STAIRCASE WERE
PAINTED BY CANADIAN
ARTIST FREDERICK
HAINES IN THE LATE
1930S AND DEPICT THE
FORMAL GARDEN AT
PARKWOOD, WHICH HAD
JUST BEEN CREATED BY
JOHN LYLE. *(JK)*

RIGHT: THREE OF THE
SILK-COVERED PANELS
THAT LINE THE
STAIRWAY WALL
CONCEAL THE AEOLIAN
ORGAN PIPES. *(JK)*

ARCHITECT JOHN
PEARSON
DECORATED
PARKWOOD IN A
SPARE, ENGLISH-
COUNTRY MANNER.
HOWEVER, WHEN
CASA LOMA'S
FURNISHINGS AND
DECORATIVE ITEMS
CAME ONTO THE
AUCTION BLOCK IN
1924, SAM AND
ADELAIDE JOINED
OTHER WEALTHY
FAMILIES TO PLACE
THEIR BIDS. AS A
RESULT, MUCH OF
PARKWOOD'S
INTERIOR REFLECTS
A MORE LAVISH AND
ECLECTIC STYLE. *(PA)*

THE DRAWING ROOM
WAS ADELAIDE'S
FAVOURITE ROOM FOR
RECEIVING GUESTS,
AND WAS
REDECORATED IN THE
1930S. IT IS BELIEVED
THAT MUCH OF THE
FURNITURE, WHICH IS
IN THE LOUIS XV
STYLE, ALONG WITH
THE CARVED WALL
PANELS, CAME FROM A
LARGE HOME IN
FRANCE. (PA)

THE BEAUTIFULLY PAINTED STEINWAY PLAYER PIANO IN THE DRAWING ROOM WAS PURCHASED AT EATON'S FOR $10,000. IT WAS SUBSEQUENTLY SENT TO HAMBURG, GERMANY, FOR DECORATIVE PAINTING. *[JK]*

"TEA was a serious event," recalls Hilda. "It took place promptly at four o'clock, every day. Two staff members would carry the tea cart down the steps, laden with tea sandwiches of cucumber, egg, fruitcakes and cookies." In warmer weather, tea would often be served under the trees by the tennis court.

The sunroom, added in the 1930s, is decorated with Chinese Chippendale furniture and features ceiling murals, *The Gods of the Wine Festival*, painted by Italian artisans. The paintings flanking the windows have been applied directly on the walls. This room was a favourite for everyday activities as well as for entertaining.

THE SUNROOM, CENTRE OF ACTIVITY IN THE McLAUGHLIN HOUSEHOLD. *(JK)*

In the 1950s, on most days, Sam and Adelaide sat down at four o'clock to a game of bridge or Scrabble with friends or staff. Anyone joining the game had to have their wits about them, especially if money was at stake. Adelaide was not only an excellent card player, but she was firm about payment of debts, no matter how small. *(JK)*

ABOVE: THE SIDE HALL, BEFORE 1924. THE HALL ADJOINS THE FOYER, DRAWING ROOM, LOGGIA, DINING ROOM AND LIBRARY, AND IS LIT BY TWO CZECHOSLOVAKIAN CHANDELIERS. THE SERIES OF MURALS WAS PAINTED IN THE 1920S BY CANADIAN ARTIST FREDERICK CHALLENER. (PA)

LEFT: *THE ENCHANTED WOOD* MURAL PORTRAYS AN ANGEL WATCHING OVER THE MCLAUGHLIN GRANDCHILDREN. IN THE CENTRE PANEL, HILDA MCLAUGHLIN PANGMAN TELLS A STORY TO HER NIECE AND NEPHEW, DIANA AND DEREK PHILLIPS, AND OTHER CHILDREN. (JK)

RIGHT: TWO PIECES OF FURNITURE GIVEN TO THE McLAUGHLINS WERE THE MORRIS-STYLE RECLINING CHAIR, AN 1898 WEDDING GIFT FROM SAM'S BROTHER JACK, AND THE LIBRARY STEPS, WHICH ALSO SERVED AS A COMMODE, A GIFT TO SAM FROM HIS DAUGHTER ISABEL. *(JK)*

BELOW: A PORTRAIT OF ADELAIDE, PAINTED FOR HER FIFTIETH BIRTHDAY, HANGS IN THE LIBRARY. *(JK)*

THE MAIDS COULD WALK THROUGH THE DINING-ROOM WALL. THE DOOR FROM THE DINING ROOM TO THE SIDE HALL SEEMS TO BLEND INVISIBLY INTO THE SILK DAMASK DINING-ROOM WALLS. STAFF COULD BE SUMMONED BY PRESSING A BUZZER AT THE HEAD OF THE TABLE. *(JK)*

THE DINING ROOM at Parkwood is a formal, spacious room. The mahogany table, when extended, can seat twenty-two. A chandelier fashioned of Bohemian glass hangs from the ceiling.

Overseeing the gatherings was Paul Peel's painting, *After the Bath*, originally owned by the Hungarian government. Sam McLaughlin bought the painting in the 1930s and it was later bequeathed to the Art Gallery of Ontario. A copy now hangs in Parkwood's dining room.

Dinner was announced promptly at 6:45 by the sound of a gong located in the side hall. Everyone was expected to arrive at the table within five minutes, to appease Sam's strong feelings about punctuality. Hilda recalls sliding down the mahogany banister "bolt upright and sidesaddle" in an attempt to arrive on time for meals.

Sam had a little slate on a china stand placed in front of him with the menu written on it, even at lunch. He would know what was to be served and would thus judge how much room to leave for dessert. Adelaide insisted on a varied menu that included lots of vegetables from the garden. The art of entertaining was honed by a refined Scottish butler, Mr. Telford Lindsay. On special occasions, young children would be seated at their own table, a miniature replica of the adults' table.

PORTRAITS OF THE MCLAUGHLIN FAMILY ADORN THE DINING-ROOM WALLS. LEFT TO RIGHT: HILDA, ISABEL AND EILEEN. ALL BUT BILLIE'S WERE DONE BY THE BRITISH ARTIST SALISBURY, WHO ALSO PAINTED PORTRAITS OF THE ROYAL FAMILY. *(JK)*

CONSIDERED BY MANY TO BE THE "NICEST" ROOM IN THE HOUSE, THE SUN-FILLED BREAKFAST ROOM FEATURES A FEATHERED MAHOGANY TABLE EDGED IN BURLED WALNUT. THE CEILING IS FINELY HAND-PAINTED IN PASTEL SHADES. (JK)

THE UPSTAIRS ART GALLERY once served as the McLaughlin daughters' playroom. Referred to as the ballroom, it housed a grand piano and one of the first Victrolas in Oshawa. As teenagers, the daughters held "tea dances" here, with food, music and dancing.

When the food needed to be replenished, the girls would draw lots to decide who would face the fierce Scottish cook, who would greet them in a thick brogue with "What'll you be wanting now?" It was this same cook who suggested "Parkwood" when the McLaughlins were looking for a good name for their new home.

THE PAINTINGS IN THIS 1978 PHOTOGRAPH BELONGED TO ISABEL MCLAUGHLIN AND WERE THEN ON EXTENDED LOAN TO PARKWOOD. THEY NOW BELONG TO THE ROBERT MCLAUGHLIN ART GALLERY IN OSHAWA. A SERIES OF CLARENCE GAGNON PAINTINGS THAT HUNG IN THE UPSTAIRS HALL OUTSIDE THIS ROOM WERE ACQUIRED BY THE MCMICHAEL GALLERY IN KLEINBURG AFTER SAM'S DEATH. (JK)

COLONEL SAM, as he is still known in Oshawa, was an honourary colonel of the local Ontario Regiment. Other titles bestowed in recognition of his support include honourary degrees from several Canadian universities and a Companion of the Order of Canada granted in 1967. He was also a generous patron of the Boy Scouts, donated Camp Samac and funded the McLaughlin Public Library, the Memorial Bandshell, Guide House, the YWCA, and additions to the Oshawa General Hospital. When Sam McLaughlin died, at the age of one hundred, in 1972, Parkwood was left to the hospital.

ORIGINALLY A SCREENED-IN PORCH, SAM'S DRESSING ROOM ADJOINS HIS BEDROOM, WHICH WAS ONCE THE SCHOOLROOM. THE SCOTTISH DRESS REGALIA LIKELY REFLECTS MCLAUGHLIN'S INTEREST IN HIS MOTHER'S HERITAGE. (JK)

SAM'S BEDROOM IS A
FINE EXAMPLE OF THE
ART DECO STYLE,
POPULAR IN THE 1930S.
THIS ROOM AND
FURNITURE, WHICH
INCLUDES TWENTY-ONE
MATCHING PIECES IN
OAK AND CHESTNUT,
WERE DESIGNED BY
JOHN LYLE.

IN HIS ONE HUNDREDTH
YEAR, SAM TOLD A
REPORTER FROM THE
OSHAWA TIMES THAT HIS
FAVOURITE PAINTING
WAS THE ONE HANGING
OVER HIS BED. IT IS
UNSIGNED AND DEPICTS
THREE POLAR BEARS ON
AN ICE FLOE. (JK)

THE GREEN ROOM, RESERVED FOR IMPORTANT GUESTS, HAS ITS OWN BATHROOM AND FIREPLACE. THIS WAS UNUSUAL IN 1917. *(JK)*

ORIGINALLY the master suite, Adelaide's bedroom was fitted with furnishings from France in the 1930s. She could summon a nurse or maid by pushing a button on a panel between the beds. When Adelaide became ill, Sam moved to his own quarters down the hall. Adelaide died in 1958, at the age of eighty-five.

ADELAIDE SPENT QUIET TIME IN HER ROOM, WRITING LETTERS AND SPEECHES, ORGANIZING NEWS CLIPPINGS, AND DOING NEEDLEWORK. A PHOTOGRAPH OF THE FIVE MCLAUGHLIN DAUGHTERS SITS ON THE ROUND TABLE IN ADELAIDE'S BEDROOM. *(JK)*

SAM ENJOYED
ENTERTAINING OLD
FRIENDS IN THE
BILLIARD ROOM ON
SATURDAY
AFTERNOONS.
ADELAIDE WAS A
SKILLFUL BILLIARDS
PLAYER AND COULD
GIVE HER HUSBAND
STIFF COMPETITION,
WINNING MORE OFTEN
THAN NOT. (JK)

THE MURALS IN THE
BILLIARD ROOM WERE
PAINTED BY
CHALLENER, AND
DEPICTED FAVOURITE
MCLAUGHLIN
ACTIVITIES. AN
ARTISAN FROM
HAMILTON, ONTARIO,
HAND-CARVED THE
FIREPLACE SURROUND,
WHICH FEATURES THE
MCLAUGHLIN COAT-
OF-ARMS IN THE
CENTRE PANEL. (JK)

"SAM LIKED TO BE BUSY," recalls former employee Betty McMullen. He exercised daily and was proud of his vitality. Ted Morrison, an Oshawa high-school principal, was a young student working in the gardens in the early 1960s, and remembers an incident when the ladies from a local TOPS (Take Off Pounds Sensibly) organization were touring the Parkwood grounds. Sam wandered out and challenged one unsuspecting lady to punch him in his mid-section. She obliged, to her own regret, and nursed a sore hand for the rest of the tour.

AN INDOOR SWIMMING POOL WAS UNUSUAL AT THE
TIME PARKWOOD WAS BUILT. ALSO LOCATED IN THE
RECREATIONAL WING ARE A SQUASH COURT
AND A BARBER SHOP. (JK)

THE BOWLING ALLEY FEATURES ONE OF THE FIRST AUTOMATIC PIN-SETTERS. THE LONG WALL WAS HUNG WITH GROUP OF SEVEN PAINTINGS, NOW IN THE McMICHAEL COLLECTION IN KLEINBURG, ONTARIO. THE McLAUGHLIN CHRISTMAS TREE WAS SET UP HERE EVERY YEAR; THE REST OF THE HOUSE WAS DECORATED FOR THE SEASON WITH PLANTS FROM THE GREENHOUSE. (JK)

FAMILY AND SOCIAL EVENTS

ABOVE ALL, PARKWOOD WAS A MUCH-LOVED HOME, enjoyed by family and friends for fifty-five years. The McLaughlins' lifestyle allowed them to entertain on a grand scale, but the ambience of a warm family life still exists at Parkwood. The amenities of the house reflect the many different interests of the family.

In the early years, horseback riding was an important focus for the McLaughlin daughters. Tennis and a full range of indoor recreational activities were available as well. Adelaide and Sam enjoyed playing a variety of games and they encouraged the girls in this pursuit.

The McLaughlins entertained many prominent political and business people, but not to the exclusion of their local friends. Starting in 1928, the McLaughlins hosted an annual November Chrysanthemum Tea, welcoming up to eight hundred guests.

THE DUKE OF
DEVONSHIRE,
GOVERNOR
GENERAL OF
CANADA, MADE A
VISIT TO
PARKWOOD IN 1919.
ADELAIDE (FAR
RIGHT), THE DUKE
OF DEVONSHIRE
(FRONT ROW, TOP
HAT), SAM (LEFT
OF THE DUKE),
SAM'S FATHER,
ROBERT (BACK,
LEFT OF SAM). *(PA)*

ABOVE: THE MCLAUGHLINS
RECEIVING GUESTS AT A GARDEN
PARTY ON THE SOUTH LAWN,
1939. LEFT TO RIGHT:
ISABEL, SAM, ADELAIDE. *(PA)*

LEFT: HILDA'S WEDDING TO JOHN
PANGMAN AT PARKWOOD, 1926. *(PA)*

SAM AND
ADELAIDE
AT THEIR
CHRYSANTHEMUM
TEA IN THE
1950S. NOTE THE
GROUP OF SEVEN
PAINTINGS, WHICH
HUNG IN THE
BOWLING ALLEY
UNTIL SAM'S
DEATH IN
1972. *(PA)*

CHRYSANTHEMUMS AND STATUE IN THE GREENHOUSE. (JK)

Chrysanthemum Tea

STEP BACK TO THE EARLY 1950S and a Saturday afternoon in the middle of November. The McLaughlins are hosting their annual Chrysanthemum Tea at their imposing Oshawa residence, Parkwood. It is a grand affair much anticipated by those in attendance. Chauffeurs are parking cars, caterers are arranging trays of food, and friends and relatives who have been asked to help have arrived early. Tea servers and assistants wear corsages to identify them as helpers. Some greet guests at the door and others serve the sandwiches, salads, and petit fours. Female friends and relatives pour tea and coffee at either end of the massive dining room table. As many as six hundred people will be greeted in a receiving line by Sam and Adelaide McLaughlin and their immediate family.

Parkwood has been decorated with magnificent bouquets of chrysanthemums. All invited are free to wander through impressive flower displays in several greenhouses and to socialize with other guests, who could include the Lieutenant Governor of Ontario, provincial cabinet ministers, a former Ontario premier and noteworthy out-of-town visitors. Local people include relatives, old friends, and business associates of Sam's. The downstairs becomes more crowded as the afternoon wears on. Some of the guests slip upstairs to the art gallery where the bar is located and smoking is permitted. Then, having visited friends and admired the flowers and wonderful surroundings, the guests filter out and most are gone by six o'clock.

LEFT: THE 1956 CHRISTMAS CARD WAS A PHOTO TAKEN ON SAM MCLAUGHLIN'S EIGHTY-FIFTH BIRTHDAY, SEPTEMBER 8, 1956, IN THE SUNDIAL GARDEN. (SEATED) HILDA, ADELAIDE, SAM. (STANDING, LEFT TO RIGHT) EILEEN, ISABEL, BILLIE, MILDRED. *(PA)*

BELOW: GOVERNOR GENERAL GEORGES VANIER AND SAM AT PARKWOOD IN THE 1960S. *(PA)*

SAM BEING DRIVEN IN A 1908 McLAUGHLIN BUICK ON HIS NINETIETH BIRTHDAY, 1961. [PA]

SAM SURROUNDED BY FAMILY AND FRIENDS ON HIS NINETY-FOURTH BIRTHDAY, 1965. *(MH)*

THE GARDENS

PARKWOOD'S GARDENS are historically significant. A succession of notable landscape architects were involved in the evolution of the property's layout over the fifty-seven-year period of McLaughlin ownership. The overall landscape consists of four areas: the South Lawn area, the formal garden area, the service area and the residential area. Within these are several distinct gardens divided by hedges.

Smaller gardens have been developed thoughtfully with a sympathetic view of the land. The Art Deco design of the Formal Garden is particularly unique in Canada. Other highlights include the Italian Garden within the residential area, the Sunken Garden in the South Lawn area, and the greenhouses within the service area. As many as twenty gardeners were employed maintaining Parkwood's grounds when the McLaughlins were in residence.

AS ILLUSTRATED IN A 1919 AERIAL PHOTOGRAPH, THE LANDSCAPE WAS OPEN, THOUGH MATURE TREES FROM THE PROPERTY'S PREVIOUS LIFE AS A PUBLIC PARK STILL GRACED THE GROUNDS. THE DESIGNERS INVOLVED FROM 1915 TO 1919 WERE LANDSCAPE ARCHITECTS W. E. HARRIES AND A. V. HALL.

TODAY A LARGE HOSPITAL PARKING GARAGE SITS ON THE NORTHWEST CORNER OF THE ESTATE WHERE THE CUTTING AND VEGETABLE GARDENS WERE LOCATED. [AO]

PARKWOOD IN 1919. OSHAWA GENERAL HOSPITAL IS VISIBLE AT TOP LEFT. THE OSHAWA HIGH SCHOOL (NOW O'NEILL COLLEGIATE) IS AT MIDDLE TOP, WITH SIMCOE STREET RUNNING BETWEEN PARKWOOD AND THE SCHOOL. GEORGE MCLAUGHLIN'S HOUSE IS VISIBLE AT EXTREME RIGHT. (AO)

PART OF AN OVERVIEW
OF THE PLAN FOR
PARKWOOD ESTATE,
DECEMBER 1931. *(PA)*

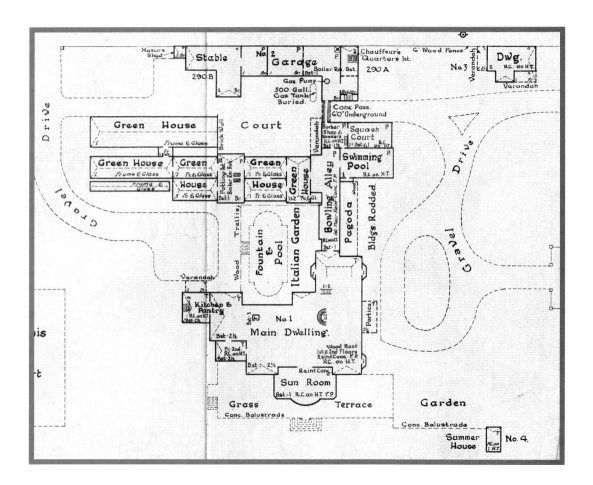

ABOVE: THE ORIGINAL GREENHOUSES AND GAZEBO, CIRCA 1919. THE GREENHOUSES WERE USED FOR ENTERTAINING, ESPECIALLY FOR THE CHRYSANTHEMUM TEA, AS WELL AS FOR GROWING FLOWERS AND PLANTS TO DECORATE THE HOUSE AND STOCK THE GARDENS. *(PA)*

RIGHT: A SERIES OF ARCHWAYS LEADING TOWARDS THE BACK OF HOUSE AND PARALLEL TO THE TENNIS COURT, 1919. *(PA)*

The southwest corner of the estate was grazing pasture for cows in 1919. During the 1920s, stables and a horse arena were constructed. These were removed in the early 1930s, leaving the area available for the development in 1935 of the Formal Garden, designed by John Lyle. *(CTA)*

A view from the South Lawn looking towards the South Terrace and house, 1919. *(PA)*

An important feature of the original landscape design is the cedar hedging, which created a privacy barrier around the estate and was used to divide the property into several distinct gardens. The Sunken Garden was designed by the Dunington-Grubbs in 1927. The influential landscape architects also were involved in the design of the South Terrace, the Sundial Garden, the tennis court and the Italian Garden. *(PA)*

55

LEFT: A GATE LEADING INTO THE ITALIAN GARDEN. (PA)

BELOW: THE ITALIAN GARDEN, LOCATED STEPS FROM THE LIBRARY, WAS DESIGNED IN THE MID- TO LATE 1920S. THE THREE GRACES STATUE AND BOY WITH GOOSE STATUE, IMPORTED FROM ITALY, STAND IN THE LILY POND, WHICH IS SURROUNDED BY A FLAGSTONE WALK AND FORMAL, SYMMETRICAL FLOWER BEDS. A CEDAR HEDGE, JUNIPER AND YEW SHRUBS ACT AS BACKDROP.

A SECLUDED SPACE ENCLOSED BY INTRICATE LATTICEWORK, THE ITALIAN GARDEN WAS DESIGNED FOR PRIVATE CONTEMPLATION AND YET WAS EASILY ACCESSED FROM THE HOUSE. (PA)

THE SOUTH TERRACE and Lawn were originally designed by Harries and Hall at the time of construction. The terrace was redesigned in 1928 by the husband and wife team, H. B. and L. A. Dunington-Grubb, and Darling and Pearson in the Arts and Crafts style. Near the house were the formal garden areas; beyond these were open lawn and, gradually, away from the house, more wooded areas.

THE SOUTH TERRACE.
THE SUMMER HOUSE IS
IN THE DISTANCE. *(PA)*

LEFT: ARCHITECT JOHN LYLE DESIGNED AND BUILT THE FORMAL GARDEN IN 1935 AND 1936. THE EAST ENTRANCE IN THE PHOTO ILLUSTRATES AN ELEVATED TERRACE WITH A FOUNTAIN DROPPING WATER INTO A POOL WITH TWO GOOSE STATUES. STAIRS ON EITHER SIDE OF THE TERRACE LEAD TO THE GARDENS. (PA)   RIGHT: A VIEW THROUGH A DECORATIVE WROUGHT-IRON GATE LOOKING EAST FROM THE TEA HOUSE TOWARDS THE FORMAL GARDEN TERRACE. (PA)

THE ART DECO LIMESTONE TEA HOUSE AT THE WEST END OF THE FORMAL GARDEN IS ENCLOSED ON THREE SIDES AND FEATURES A KITCHEN, WASHROOM AND CLOAKROOM, MAKING IT CONVENIENT FOR ENTERTAINING. THE SEVEN-FOOT-TALL STONE URNS RECESSED IN BAY NICHES MAKE A DRAMATIC ACCENT. THIS AREA NOW SERVES AS A SUMMER RESTAURANT. (AO)

A REFLECTIVE MOMENT IN THE TEA HOUSE. *(PA)*

SAM AND ADELAIDE
MCLAUGHLIN RELAXING
IN THE TEA HOUSE OF
THE FORMAL GARDEN. *(PA)*

BIBLIOGRAPHY

Aldwinckle, Jo. *Oshawa General Hospital "Heart-beat of the Community."* Oshawa: The Alger Press, 1975

EDA Collaborative Inc. "Landscape Conservation Study for Parkwood Estate." September 1998. Parkwood Archives.

Hunter, Robert. "Agenda Paper for Historic Sites and Monuments Board of Canada." Oshawa: Parkwood, 1990. Parkwood Archives.

Illustrated Historical Atlas of the County of Ontario, Ont. Toronto: J. H. Beers & Co., 1877.

McLaughlin Henderson, Dorothy. *Robert McLaughlin Carriage Builder*, Toronto: Griffin Press Limited, 1972.

McLaughlin, R. S., as told to Erin Hutton. "My Eighty Years on Wheels," *Maclean's,* 15 September, 1 October, 15 October 1954.

"The McLaughlins' Chrysanthemum Tea." *Mayfair,* February 1950.

"My First Century on Wheels." *Weekend Magazine,* 13 November 1971.

Oshawa Times, McLaughlin Public Library.

Parks Canada. "Parkwood National Historic Site Commemorative Integrity Statement." September 1998. Parkwood Archives.

Parkwood tour guide script, compiled by Parkwood staff and volunteers.

Robertson, Heather. *Driving Force.* Toronto: McClelland & Stewart Inc., 1995.

ACKNOWLEDGMENTS

We are particularly grateful to Bradley Lockner for his support and editorial guidance.

We'd especially like to thank Marion O'Donnell for her recollections and hours of help with photograph retrieval at Parkwood. Mary Hare and Nancy Miller generously shared their recollections and lent photographs. We appreciate the loan of negatives from the talented Dr. James Kwan, who took many of the interior photographs. Special thanks also to Hilda Pangman, daughter of Colonel Sam, for sharing her memories with us.

Our sincere thanks go to the staff at Parkwood, in particular Kathy Kidman, Nancy Lawrence, Brian Malcolm and summer students Andrew Morin and Theressa Smith.

We'd also like to thank Sylva Armstrong, Ron Bouckley, Elizabeth McMullen, Ron Lace, Donald O'Leary, Marg Pellow and Tammy Robinson.

Thanks to our husbands Myles and Chris and to our children Nathaniel and Jordan Beatty and Graham and Fraser Hall for their love and support. Lastly, thanks to Georgia Taylor for planting the seed.

DONORS

We are grateful to the following organizations and individuals for their financial contributions.

Bradley and Charlene Lockner

Parkwood Foundation

Parkwood Volunteers

PHOTO CREDITS

Archives of Ontario (AO)

Canadian Automotive Museum Inc. (CAM)

City of Toronto Archives (CTA)

Mary Hare (MH)

James Kwan (JK)

McLaughlin Library, Oshawa Public Library (ML)

Nancy Miller (NM)

Oshawa General Hospital Archives (OGH)

Parkwood Archives (PA)